EVERY POEM A POTION,
EVERY SONG A SPELL

STEPHANIE PARENT

Every Poem a Potion,
Every Song a Spell

Querencia Press, LLC

Chicago Illinois

QUERENCIA PRESS

© Copyright 2023
Stephanie Parent

ISBN 978 1 959118 38 1

www.querenciapress.com

First Published in 2023

Querencia Press, LLC
Chicago IL

Printed & Bound in the United States of America

CONTENTS

Foreword 9

When Everything Else Was Gone 15

Into the Forest 17

Part One: Strange Creatures..19

Crack Nuts...21

Stepsisters 23

Red Hood in the Woods..25

Clawed Creatures 27

Little Cages 31

Poissonnier 33

Part Two: Little Houses..35

Twice Fooled..37

Little Bones 39

Marlene 41

Gretel..43

No Dumb Bunny 46

The House on Chicken Legs 49

Boy, Lost 51

Snegurochka..53

Part Three: Wild Gardens 55

Rampion 58

The Hanging Garden 60

Amphibious Love 62

Silver and Stone 64

Walnut Heart.. 66

Dream Garden.. 68

Thorns and Wings 70

Part Four: Enchanted Castles....................................... 72

Curse of the Firstborn 74

Skin and Salt... 76

Eternity... 79

Blessed Curse 82

Too Late or Never 84

Invisible Bars 86

Epilogue: Disenchanted 89

Uncaged 91

The Question... 94

The Answer 96

Notes on Previous Publications 99

Foreword

I began writing this poetry collection while I was working on a long nonfiction project, a personal story that drew symbolism from fairy tales in their oldest, darkest forms. As a child I had read older versions of fairy tales in Andrew Lang's *Colored Fairy Books*, in picture books with illustrations by Kay Nielsen and Arthur Rackham, and in a treasured volume titled *Clever Gretchen and Other Forgotten Folktales*, edited by Alison Lurie. I also watched the Disney princess movies more times than I could count, knew the princesses' ballads and love songs by heart, and carried glass figurines of Ariel and Aurora with me to school and displayed them on my bedroom shelves.

I adored the original fairy tales with their shades of blood and shadow, their echoes of violence and loss, lingering among the happy endings. I loved the modern versions with their Technicolor heroines, their stories of sacrifice rewarded and true love conquering all. In my child's mind, the two types of tales melded, till I believed no happily-ever-after was possible without the undercurrent of human cruelty and a cold, uncaring world. What were fairy godmothers and witches, after all, but two sides of the same coin? Couldn't magic lose its power if we found it without first plunging to the depths of adversity?

While working on my nonfiction project, I was disappointed to realize how many modern readers knew only of the Disney fairy tales. They weren't familiar with the original *Little Mermaid,* where with every step the mergirl took on dry land, invisible knives impaled her feet, or the version of *Snow White and the Seven Dwarves* where the evil queen danced to her death in red-hot shoes. They had never read the tales of clever girls who made their own fate, like *Kate Crackernuts*, or the haunting stories of characters trapped in cages of every type, like *Jorinda and Joringel.* Trying to distill the essence of these tales, to explain them to readers while also telling my own story, was difficult, so I channeled my frustration into a project I began only for myself: this book of poems.

As this collection of poems developed, and as it became too big to be written for my eyes only, I penned poems inspired by both well-known and more obscure tales. Even for the most familiar stories, I drew on details left out of the sanitized modern versions. In some cases I retold an entire tale, in others just a portion of it. In some poems I used the fairy tale to explore my personal experience, while in others I described characters I could relate to, but whose perspectives were very different from my own. Some poems referenced our modern world, while others remained firmly in the realm of a once-upon-a-time past. Some focused on magic, others on the mundane.

Despite the different approaches, all these poems contain something of me in them, and all comment on the experience of being human—and, often, a woman—in a magical and cruel world. After all, fairy tales were stories traditionally told by and to women, reflecting and sometimes questioning standards of femininity, whispering secrets about how to survive real-life beastly husbands and evil stepmothers between the lines of an imagined tale.

I've included the name of each fairy-tale inspiration below the title of its poem, in the hopes that some readers might be inspired to search out stories they've never read or have long forgotten, or to read an older version of a familiar tale. Of course, you can also enjoy the poems on their own, and make your own meaning from the stories and symbols within them—just as readers, listeners and re-tellers of fairy tales have done for so long.

When Everything Else Was Gone

When my friends wouldn't pick up the phone
And the memories of a lover's limbs beside me
Had faded from fire to
Smoke

When my free hours had been consumed by
Teaching and typing on computers
And still my bank account kept dwindling
And my bills kept multiplying
And my earnings slipped like bitter salt
Between my fingers

When my mind had no more room for
Dreams of flight and freedom
Amid all the worry weighing me down
                              down
                                    down

When I looked in the mirror and saw only
The angry red trails of my suffering
Written across my skin

When I had lost everything
I once believed I
Possessed

I had only this:

A blank piece of paper
And the memory of a book of fairy tales

Girls who walked barefoot through the snow
Girls who wove cloth fine enough to fit through the eye
Of a needle

Girls who found the treasure within
A million grains of rice

Girls who discovered
Hidden within themselves

> (Within bodies that had become maps of
> Damage and disappointment)

The key to their own
Salvation

Into the Forest

What is it about the woods?

Even whispering the word—

…woods, woods, woods…

Conjures scraped knees, ripped dresses
Pounding hearts
Secrets and monsters and
Salvation

Fairy tales tell us
We all have a forest within us

Men might march through
With axes and torches

But women slip sidewise
Through the branches
Welcoming fear and shadow
As familiar friends

We know what we're running from:
Evil stepmothers
Fathers with monstrous demands
Demon bridegrooms
And fairy curses

(don't touch the spindle
don't go out in the sunlight
don't grow up and become too
beautiful—but not too ugly either—
never dare to become too much
for the world to bear)

These curses still exist
Though the names they go by
Have become mundane

(*stress and anxiety
disappointment
despair*)

With each tree chopped down
Each forest annihilated
And concrete castle erected
Another magic wand
Snaps
Like twigs beneath bare feet

Doesn't matter—the trees live
In our minds
Branches and brain nerves
Aren't so different
And behind every logical choice

(*go to college
start a savings account
find a nice boy*)

Lies a memory of the deep scent
Of soil and blood
Lingering like the memory
Of something dangerous
On the edge of lost

Part One: Strange Creatures

I never wanted to be a human girl
Who sweated under her arms
Grew prickly hairs on her legs
Bled between her thighs

I wanted to be a mermaid
Scaled and sleek
My fishtail a blue-green
As deep
As the ocean floor
Where the light doesn't
Reach

I wanted to be a fairy
A tiny, precious thing
My wings
As fragile
As lace, or as the web of a
Fallen leaf

I wanted to be a dryad
Slender as the branch of a willow

A naiad
Silky as a stream that sings
Its way between the trees

> (Or if I couldn't be any of these things
> I wanted to be one of those girls with
> Cascading hair, poreless skin, careless
> Laughs—the ones that walked out of a
> Fairy tale or shampoo commercial, and made
> Me feel, beside them, something
> Other

Inferior
Unable to hide my
Deficiencies)

But there I was—
A flawed, human girl
With all the odors and heavy flesh and discharge
That being human brings
And when I came too close to another
We repelled each other
like two magnets

So instead I sought the woods
And the creatures that might slip from my mind
From my dreams
To creep along the branches
To fly above the forest
And lie in wait for me
Among the trees

Crack Nuts
Kate Crackernuts

When I left home for the first time
Flew across the country to graduate school
Like a girl fleeing toward
The sorcery between the branches
Which had to be better than what she left behind—

When I left home for the first time
I went a little nuts

I didn't find the castles or cottages or huntsmen I hoped for
In my forest, which was actually a city
Bordered by salty oceans and ashy mountains

And since my mother
Was incorporeal
On the other side of a cell phone signal
It seemed safe to tell her
Of my disappointment, and the idea
That had entered my head

"Don't you ever dare do that to me," she said

It was not what I wanted to hear

"You must really be hurting," I had hoped for
And perhaps she said that too, on a different phone call
But my mind chose to recall
What it chose to recall

I felt like someone had cast a spell on me
Replaced my face with a sheep's head
Prickly wool swathed my eyes and ears
Rubbed my skin raw

Separated me from sanity

I had to wrap myself in layers
Conceal my bizarre affliction
Everywhere I went
And wait for someone stronger and braver
Than I could ever be
To crack nuts
And crack the curse

Stepsisters
Kate Crackernuts, Part Two

Shame sits hot and sticky beneath her skin
Knowing the truth of her bloodline
Knowing her own mother—not stepmother—
Believed she wanted this

Wanted her dearest, her other half
To wear a sheep's head

In another world, Kate and Ann might have been lovers
They grew up together, curled like commas in the same bed
Tender, innocent flesh pressed close enough
To keep warm when the covers were threadbare

Two sheep in a flock
Shielding each other from the wolves
Who ruled over their tiny kingdom

In this world, Ann lost her beauty, her hope
Hid her wooly head behind layer upon layer
Of coarse fabric, like a supplicant
While Kate
Let shame boil into anger, hot enough to leap
From the witch's pot

Anger that her mother had done this to them both
Had sickened her sister
Had left Kate to toil tirelessly
To make up for the wrongs in her bloodline

Anger made Kate sit up all night
Beside the prince's bedside

Anger made her follow the prince

Inside the fairy mound

Anger made her vision clear as glass
So she saw not the fairies' gossamer wings
Not their long lithe limbs
But their cruel hearts
Like her mother's cruel heart

Anger turned to fury
As Kate stole the fairy bird
Soaked its golden feathers in ruby blood
A jeweled offering

Fed it like her own tender flesh
To the prince she settled for
Though her heart would always belong to
Her sister

In soul if not
In blood

Red Hood in the Woods
Little Red Riding Hood

Look: She wouldn't have worn red
If she didn't want the wolf to notice her.
Right?

Like the teenage girl strolling down the street
On a hot summer's day
White bra straps slipping from her sundress
Pink tongue peeking out
Slinking around a strawberry popsicle

Or the twenty-something at the club on a Saturday night
Skintight black dress, pomegranate-seed-red stilettos
Hips unmoored from decorum
Beneath the splash of the spotlights

Asking for it

So what?

So what if we did choose the shortcuts
Through the woods, down the alley
Across that vacant lot after midnight
Off the path
Where the wild things prowl
To the beat of our wild hearts

We asked for the bite of the wind
Like incisors
Across our bare legs

We asked for the slither of a moonbeam
Like claws
Across our bare shoulders

We didn't ask to be trapped
Within the rank flesh
Of the wolf's belly
Tucked into ourselves, knees kissing temples
Breathing blood and acid and fear
Waiting for some huntsman to slit the fur
See that red hood
Like a scream, as if color were a sound
And tug our cramped, cornered bodies
Back out

Clawed Creatures
Beauty and the Beast

She entered the woods in autumn
The leaves dangled from the trees
Red as a woman's first blood
They fluttered to the earth and the wind stirred them
With a hollow song
Like the whisper of old bones

The leaves rustled and parted before her feet as she walked
And walked
Till her boots grew threadbare and the mud
Seeped through
And froze along with the leather beneath it
Stiff and cracked
Cold air
Tickling her toes

Winter came while she was still walking
Snow snuck in, white blossoms blooming
In an indigo sky
Silencing the song of the leaves
Coating the bare bones of the trees
The world still and expectant as a held breath

***

Last spring, her father had arrived home
Holding a rose with petals the color of blood—
A rose that never withered
Though the frost still crunched beneath his boots
The half-frozen gate still creaked on its hinges
As he stepped back into his bedraggled garden
Telling tales of a monster
That no one quite believed

But when spring sprung into summer
The sun merciless, the grass bleached dry
And still that rose pulsed red as a beating heart
His words didn't seem quite so strange

And when autumn arrived
And her father's cough grew into something
Monstrous
Phlegm and snot and a sound like a broken rattle
Beauty knew she would have to find this monster
With his bewitched garden
And ask his forgiveness

**

As she treks through the snow
Seeing the spires of the Beast's castle rise
In the distance, Beauty wonders:
Is she really trying to save her father?
Is she truly so selfless?
Or is she the one who is
Fleeing
Hoping for a more colorful
Bloom
Than the world she left behind?

**

In the Beast's castle, it is always winter
Snow swirls round the ruby roses in a frenzy
A whirling dervish
Inside, everything is quiet and still
It's hard to tell whether she's been here a day
Or a year
It's not what she expected

She sees the Beast only by the light of candelabras
Dripping cherried wax
She sees him on the other side of a long table
The curls and whorls of his dark fur
The claws wrapping round the stem of a wineglass
Tapping a tattoo on the crimson tablecloth

She smells him
Musky and dangerous
The scent creeps into her dreams
She doesn't run from it

In the short daylight hours, she wanders
The gardens
Watches the woods from the corner of her eye
She wonders if the Beast is inside them
Hunting
And whether he moves on two feet or four

One afternoon, when the sun is slanting low
And the cold wind sneaks up her cloak
Under her skirts and between her legs
She hears a rustle in the trees
A clatter of claws

But when the Beast parts the branches
He is on two feet
Dressed in his overcoat
Only a few drops of blood
Stain his silk collar

He holds a dead rabbit
Limp and pathetic, it should wring Beauty's heart
Dry
But her pulse beats stronger

The slow, steady thud of a predator

The Beast enters the garden
Lays the rabbit at Beauty's feet
Looks up at her with eyes blue and human
As a summer sky

"Spring is coming," he says in a voice
That sounds like icicles falling to the earth
Shattering into shards
And melting as the ground finally
Thaws

Little Cages
Jorinda and Joringel, Part One

Seven hundred cages, or seven thousand
Depending on which version you read

Seven-something lovely little traps
Like Christmas ornaments
Dangling from the ceiling
In a dank and dismal chamber
Where the light could never reach

Was that why the witch collected them—
Because she yearned for light?

> (her singing birds
> transformed by her own hands
> to resemble creatures native to exotic
> worlds
> she could never see)

Who could know—

She is one of those witches too
Wild
Her cruel ways too strange
To understand and therefore
To redeem

What, then, of those maidens
Who wandered too close to the spell-caster's castle
Each one caught the sound of birdsong, girlsong
Escaping out the high barred window
And heard something of herself

No girl ends up in a beautiful cage

Without some part of her wanting it
Yearning for it, even
A difficult truth to hear

Especially for the girls
Who remember their imperfect human forms
Dull, compared to their newfound feathers
What meaning have green eyes or blue
Brown locks or golden
Beside the thousand shades
Of a winged bird's plumage

So what if they can only fly
In circles behind the bars
They count their journey
In multiples of seven

They sing, more beautiful than they ever were
Though their voices are hoarse, their throats
Tender, shards of metal behind
Each pure note
Of a song without words

They marvel at how long they must wait
For rescue to come

Poissonnier
The Little Mermaid

How much must you scorn yourself
To desire to cleave yourself
In two
And hope someone will notice
The new creature you've become?

Or perhaps it is an act of love
To make your outsides match your insides
Show the world something split and broken
Descaled, ripped open
Accept the stab of metal blades
With every step on dry land
Slick rocks, grit sand, soft grass—

All knives

Our human legs are things of violence

They kick and scramble and open wide

Underwater you were safe
Surrounded by waves that rocked you to sleep
A fetus, an embryo

Safe everywhere but within your mind
Where desires woke from their slumber
Like an undertow
Dragging you
Into the most dangerous places

Wanting things you could not possess
Wanting love,
But what is love

If not pain?
What is love,
If not a split, an opening
An offering of yourself to be
Ruptured
In the hopes that someone will see the wound
And fill you?

Love is not like a fish's tail
Slippery scales that fly you through the waves
With no boundaries, no broken bits, no fears

Love is an anchor
Too heavy to lift on your own
Love is a cry in a raw throat
When you have given up your voice

Love is something you lose
It slips out of your grasp with the knowledge that
Perhaps
You never possessed it at all

Love is something that leaves behind
An echo you can't see
Though you hear it singing you to sleep

A whisper soft
As sea foam
And as hard to hold

Part Two: Little Houses

She wanted to be
Something more than what she came from
Couldn't bear a life as small
As that cottage at the edge of the woods
Cramped with dust and must that
Invaded her brain cells
Worked its way through her veins
Altered her chemistry
Till her organs tightened
Constrained by those crisscrossing wood beams
Of the cottage
A net, a web
Hemming her in on all sides

Her parents had worked hard
When they were young
And childless

Her father had chopped the trees
And stacked the wood
Arranged the puzzle pieces of a home

Her mother had polished the stove
And scrubbed the windows
Till the sun shone through like melting butter

They pretended the home was more than just
A puzzle of wood pieced together with hope
And wind singing through the cracks

But something had changed—the years
Without children, the stillborns
The way that forest at the edge of the yard
Blunted the light

For most of the year

The dust had crept out from the corners
Across the floor
And by the time the girl arrived
She was too late
Overdue
The wish granted after the wisher
Had forgotten hope

She had to hold all expectations inside herself
Light so bright it burned
And by the time she'd grown tall
The fire licking at her insides
Was burden enough to turn love and duty
To resentment

A flame that bled the candlewax
Down
Made a lump
Sticky as sap
A congealed trap
For fallen flies

By the time
The candle burnt
Out

The only fire left
Was the urge to
Run

Twice Fooled
Jorinda and Joringel, Part Two

Two villages, two sets of cottages
Little prisons made of stones stacked one atop the other
The gaps between them barely big enough
To let the buildings breathe

The gaps between each cottage, the opposite—
Chasms
Terrain too vast and treacherous to cross
No matter how sweet it looks in spring
When the wild bluebells bloom

The first time:
Joringel in one cottage, Jorinda in the other
The space between Joringel and the lovely girl

                    (Jorinda, with eyes the color of a robin's
                    egg, hair as red as that bird's breast)

A space measured in tasks and time:

The cows that need milking
The fields that need plowing
The garden that needs weeding

The wildflowers that need plucking
So he'll have an excuse to sneak away
A gift to offer

Soon, the two sneak off together
A new terrain
To cross
They flee to the woods, the shadows

But the darkness is deeper than they
Imagined

It doesn't go like they planned

A girl grows wings
Only to find herself caged

A boy escapes the forest
But leaves his heart behind
In the fathomless center
Of the woods

Little Bones
The Juniper Tree, Part One

(My mother, she killed me)

Outside the cottage grows a juniper tree
Where his mother's bones rest
Beneath branches with leaves like needles
Berries the color of the grayest skies

Inside the cottage, his stepmother stews
In her jealousy
She knows her husband's heart belongs
To those bones beneath the tree
She sees the loss shade his eyes the color
Of sour berries

So she lays a trap

(My father, he ate me)

Father, Father, *why?*

From his stepmother he expects cruelty
But from his father he finds ignorance
The greater sin
The patriarch who turns a blind eye
To all but his own aching heart
The father who doesn't question
Why the meat tastes so bittersweet
And where his son has gone

(My sister Marlene, gathered all my bones)

She cries a river of tears
Till the soup needs no salt

(Tied them in a silken scarf)

Child's bones
Become bird bones
Hollow enough to float
To fly

(Laid them beneath the juniper tree)

She knows the power
Of a dead mother's wish
Alchemy, necromancy
Strange bloom come from blood
And salt

With his hollow bird bones
And his fragile feathers
And his pure, clear voice
The boy speaks the truths
He never could before

The boy born from a wish
Made beneath a juniper tree

A wish of snow
And blood

Death

And love

Marlene
The Juniper Tree, Part Two

Who granted you a name, when your brother has none?

Certainly you deserve one, after all you've lived through—

Watching your brother's head
Roll off
Because you tapped him on the ear
As though you'd tugged the branches of the trees
Just a little too hard
And apples and pears came tumbling
Down to rot

Why did you have to ask for that apple?

Its skin was shiny as blood
Its flesh as white as your brother's pale neck
You should have known no good could come of it

You watched your family

          (what was left of it)

Go on as if nothing was wrong
The way so many families do
As if the floor wasn't littered with body parts
As if the blood hadn't seeped through the stone

You became the bearer of burdens
A pocketful of bones

          They stung like salt
          On open wounds

Your brother sang your courage
And dried your tears
But he couldn't drown out the sound

Of bones singing their darker song

Clittering and clattering
Like memories clutched
In your palm

Gretel
Hansel and Gretel

Who do I love:

My breadcrumb brother or my witch mother?

The candy house was a trap, the witch said

        —storybook witch
        warts on her nose and
        boils on her toes—

A trap for *him*, she said
She would kill *him* and cook *him* and
Eat *him*

        —loveless witch
        daughterless witch—

The witch did not feed me
Cakes and confections
Perhaps she feared temptation
The sight of my fattening flesh
That was not the fate she intended
For me

As she did for my brother

I tried to save him
I slipped him a bird bone
To replace his own finger
When the witch's nail-claws
Wrapped round it

I told him not to gorge himself

43

Still, I watched him grow wide and heavy and slow
Plodding the confines of his cage
The grotesque on show
While I shrunk

I wondered, in the world out there
Would I always be
Small
A bird scrounging for crumbs

I wondered
Would the witch teach me
How to fly like those birds perched
On the frosted roof of her cottage

How to ensnare men
And all their appetites

I wondered
Was the witch's pockmarked face
Her withered limbs
Beneath her greasy cloak
Just a disguise

Was this all a test
To see how long I could remain
How much I hungered
Whether I could be trusted

My stepmother had never touched me
Never loved me
But the witch—

Sometimes, when I'd finished my chores
She laid a hand on my bony wrist

Her fingers gentle as
Feathers
Drifting to earth

I kept a close watch
On the witch's eyes

Sometimes, I thought I saw wisdom
Deep brown as the bark of an old tree

Sometimes, I saw yearning
The blue of a wandering stream

But in the end, when the witch peered into the cage
Where my fat brother lay
I saw jealousy and greed
The same shade as my stepmother's eyes

I knew neither choice was the right one

I knew what I had to do

I gathered all my strength
The last crumbs of sugar in my veins
I pushed the witch's bony body into the fire
And left her for the flames

No Dumb Bunny
Snow White and the Seven Dwarfs

In the little log cabin
Deep in the womb of the woods
With the seven little men who were not men
She was safe

—Or thought she was
When the little men
                    (who were not men)
Left for the mines
To unearth their precious jewels—

After all, the sun was shining
The fire popped and crackled in the hearth
She'd scrubbed the cooking pot till it gleamed
And swept all the dirt from the floor
And outside the clothes on the line fluttered
Like happy ghosts in the breeze
While the bunnies fluffed as dandelion puffs
Hopped beneath

All that work, an offering
What could she hope for, in return?

The dwarves would be home before dark
Just enough time
For the papery old woman
To hang her paper hand
On the fence's gate
To set down her basket of wares and
Look right at Snow
With a smile that could melt

Just enough time

For the woman to lace Snow's bodice
With ribbons the color of blood, of lips, of roses
Her paper hands still trembling
Till that last moment, when she pulled tight—

Snow didn't notice
She was looking for something
In the old woman's eyes
And trying to decide
Whether they were brown or blue

The dwarves came home just as the last breath
Was escaping Snow's red lips
The bunnies had retreated to their burrows
The birds had ceased their song

But Snow's hope did not escape

Next morning, the men who were not men
Left again
And Snow wondered if another
Kinder visitor might arrive

She did—
Another old woman
With eyes the soft blue of the stream
That meandered just outside the cabin

How could such a woman
Bring anything but soft, sweet life?

She offered Snow a comb
Clutched in her spun-wool hands
And Snow hoped for the feeling of those hands
Stroking her hair softly
Lovingly

She got the poison comb instead

That night, the dwarves revived her
The bunnies looked on with button eyes
Snow gazed beyond the gate and saw
The dark edge of danger in the sky

But in the morning, the sun was butter
Melting all the gloom
So when the third old woman came
With eyes the brown of wise tree trunks
That have stood tall and offered
Shelter and shade
Snow took the apple from that whorled wood hand
Without a thought
She bit into the woman's gift, her love
To take it inside herself

Even as she tasted the bitter beneath the sweet
Snow knew, she knew, she knew

Snow was no dumb bunny
She was simply a girl
Full of desire
And hope
Waiting to be filled

The House on Chicken Legs
Baba Yaga/Vasilisa the Beautiful

Her cottage prowls the forest
On legs of rubbery flesh
Clacking bones
Prehistoric claws

It leaves footprints large enough
To swallow a girl
Hood and boots and all

Don't bother to follow the tracks—

The house finds you

And when you reach it
Baba Yaga will beckon you inside
The birch tree by the door will tear at your flesh
The dog will nibble at your cold ankles
The cat will scratch your thin wrist

Yaga will demand the impossible
To separate the seeds of millet
The peas and the poppy seeds

But such a task is not so difficult
For one who lives in a world
Of cruel stepmothers
Jealous sisters and
Forgetful fathers

You have been separating peas from poppy seeds
All your life

And when your eyes burn

From hours squinting in the dark
With only candlelight to guide you

When the scratches on your skin smart
And your limbs grow heavy as tree trunks

When you hear those chicken legs
Rustling beneath your feet
And feel the floor thrum

When the house runs
And carries you away
From everything you've ever known

When the old witch snores, and it sounds
Like a cackle
Like the sound she will make
Once she's devoured you

A voice you carry in your pocket
Will whisper:

Morning is wiser than evening

And a light that burns
Inside a skull
Is still a light

And you will go on

Boy, Lost
Jorinda and Joringel, Part Three

Here is Joringel, without Jorinda
In another little village
And another little house
Though in this place
No wildflowers grow

On the outside, he appears to move freely
His limbs are strong; they chop trees
Whittle wood
Forge metal
Craft weapons

But inside, he suspects
The witch's enchantment
Still holds

Inside, he is stone
His heart solid
Blood congealing
Impotent
Gone cold

He doesn't see
The young women in this village
Their gazes blue-green and bright
Working in their families' gardens
Drawing water from the wells

He doesn't see
The years passing
Winter's frost and summer's swelter
Are all the same to him

He sees
An enchanted bird in a cage
Feathers red as a
Robin's breast
And blue as the eggs
It lays

He sees the girl
He left behind
Transformed
Winged, now, but never to
Fly

He sees the girl trapped by
His cowardice like
Iron bars, a cage in the witch's castle
Blotting out the colors
Beneath

Snegurochka
The Snow Maiden

Strange how quickly you re-acclimate
After ten years melting in the sun
Of the West Coast
Your muscles remember the cold of the East
How to tighten and tremble and eventually
Soften
Accepting discomfort
And loss

Like the Snow Maiden, born to that lonely couple
In their lonely cottage
In a land where white flakes blanket the earth
For half the year
She grew out of the couple's warmth, their desire
Their love
A spark that ignited her into life
But a part of her always belonged
To the cold

You too were born of a couple's desire
For love
That red, fiery thing they'd never had enough of
Didn't know how to offer
In a way that didn't take and take
And leave you shivering

So you ran

So the Snow Maiden ran, with her friends
In the midsummer heat
She leapt over the bonfire
The flames stole her away
Consumed her human spark

And left only the mist that was her essence
Evanescent

So you, too, leapt over bonfires
Till the flames burned too bright
Blistered your skin
And you had to retreat
To that house in the East
Where the desire for love had birthed you

Too much love, too much warmth
A flame trapped in a hearth—

You couldn't release your own fiery tongues
Of desire
Couldn't retreat into your own
Bitter ice

And now, in a winter you remember
Wishing you could forget
You let the ice coat your bones
You abandon the memory of sun-warmed sand
You know, no matter how far you've tried to run
How high you've leapt
How deeply you've yearned

You can never outrun your birthright
            (Birth burden)
As someone else's story
Someone else's wish

You don't want to evaporate, like the girl
Who came to life from the snow

As long as you live, a part of you
Always belongs to the cold

Part Three: Wild Gardens

You always were different from other girls

You thought you'd be like Belle
Beautiful in your blue dress
Needing only your books and enchanted
Furniture and a fluffy little dog

        —and your beast, of course—

But the beast you found
Frightened you too much

          (the way he gnawed at your heart
          from the inside out)

So you retreated to the woods and
Wandered till your blue dress
Was stained and torn

In a picture book
You might look lovely
Like Cinderella in
Tatters, kneeling before the
Crushed orange glow of a pumpkin

          —but in real life
          that rotten fruit
          stunk

You stunk

Of soil and swamp, of sweat and dreams gone
Cold

And you began to wonder
If you were not meant to be like Belle
Or Ella or Ariel
At all

If you were destined to be different
In another way

To live apart

To abandon your dress, now rags, and
Your dreams of being desired

To dig into the earth, because you wanted
So badly to become part of it, but were
Afraid to take that final
Plunge

To ravage the soil till the dirt crept under
Your fingernails

To leave behind a part of
Yourself

To weather the winter with no
Little dog, no magic, no
Lover, only the hope that
Spring would return and with it
That part of yourself buried beneath
The earth

Would bloom, a garden, the closest
You can come to beauty
Now

(to wait
is a sort of
witchcraft

you hope it will be
enough)

Rampion
Rapunzel

Young woman with a ravaged belly
Demanding, demanding, while the child within is
Only embryo

She climbs walls, fights brambles
Desperate for nourishment
Tears leaves from the earth
Dirt under her fingernails
Devours it all, vegetable and mineral
Like a feral animal

Not even birthed yet, the babe in her belly
Has consumed her
She is too young, too tender
More blossom than stalk
Such a violent burden
Would surely destroy her

Relief
When the garden's owner claims
The greatest price
For the woman's greed

> (Greed that never belonged to her
> Anyway)

A babe so gluttonous
Needs a witch to lock her in a tower
Bind her hair
Deny her power

What else would this babe, now grown
Have ravaged

Had she walked through the world with
Tresses loose
Hands grasping
Eyes open?

She would have taken
Much more than a prince's sight

Better the tower, the stone
Where no soil births leaves with their
Nourishment dearer than
Diamonds

Dangerous growth, long locks, emerald vines

Chop it all down

Or so the young woman who's lost her babe,
The old witch who's lost her youth,
The maiden who's lost her choice,
Her voice,

All tell themselves

The Hanging Garden
Jorinda and Joringel, Part Four

Jorinda has joined the hanging garden
A barren place: soil-less, waterless
Flower-less, sunless—

It is the sun she misses
Most of all

The absence of its warmth
Is the absence of Joringel's
Touch

That boy was hot-blooded, his
Passion penetrating till she was
Certain it was love

Now, when the witch visits her hanging
Garden, her collection of cages containing
Birds who once were girls
The crone cackles about the young men
She's turned to stone

Jorinda fears her lover is among them
The fire of his blood forever chilled

Was she a fool to follow him into the woods?
Were the flames she felt in his gaze
(His hands)
Ever real?

Did Jorinda, by dreaming of
Fire and freedom, seal her
Fate—

To gain wings at last
Only within
A cage?

Amphibious Love
The Frog Prince

You've got to kiss a lot of frogs
They all told us
But some of us preferred to spend our days
Alone
By the untroubled blue water of a pond
Playing with our golden baubles
And if we dropped them in that crystalline water
We plucked them out ourselves

The comfort of dreams
Summer afternoons with the sun's rays
Stroking our hair, painting our skin
Gold
Brushing over our flaws
So much safer and simpler than
Slimy amphibian flesh against
Our own

We ignored the frogs' calls
The strange sadness behind their croaking songs
We lingered in the garden till the sun
Fled
Till the glow on our skin faded
And the old marks rose again

Suddenly we were shivering

We clutched our golden baubles
And saw that other, more practical girls
Had made princes of web-footed creatures
Transformed
Under the pale echo of the moon

We shrugged—what else could we do?—
And made our long, lonely way
Home

Silver and Stone
The Maiden Without Hands

For seven years the king fought wars
In distant lands
And dreamed of his wife with her silver hands
And the first time he saw her
Her pearl teeth closing around the flesh of the pear
That grew from his garden, his land

Back then, she had no silver appendages
When she stole pears from the king's garden
Biting the low-hanging fruit
Like an animal
Her long neck tipping upward
An offering
Witnessed—or so she
Believed—only by the moon

An offering
Like the hands she'd laid
Before her father who
Chopped
Through the wrists, where the blue veins
Shone through
Till the blood ran like a red river
And she followed it away from her home
That was no longer a home
And the father
Who was her kin no more

The king caught sight of her
In the garden he owned
A pale, midnight specter
Graceful and feral
He glimpsed the porcelain column of her neck

The stumps bound behind her back
And thought not of blood and rupture
But of precious silver
Something fragile
Meant for safekeeping

She was just another creature
Roaming his kingdom
A sleek fox, a winged dove
He loved her outside of words, of reason
Something he could tame with silver parts

Whenever he kissed her, he tasted ripe pears
And for those seven long years as he rode horses and
Led armies and
Slaughtered enemies
He closed his eyes and saw silver fingers
And savored fruit flesh on his tongue

But when he returned, and wandered the woods
Till he found his love again
The silver he'd fashioned for her was gone
In its place, slender human digits
Nimbler than any wild creature's

He would never possess her again

The disappointment sang silver on his tongue
As rocks fell from his heavy heart
And he clung tight to his human wife
Her human hands caressed
His tired flesh
Like water slipping
Down a stone

Walnut Heart
Thumbelina

A tiny poem for a tiny girl
For her, one blossom in one pot
Made a garden
And one water lily on a pond
Was a raft adrift on an endless
Ocean

A lonely woman wished Tiny
Into existence

A toad wished for a tiny companion
For her warty son

A mouse wished for a girl
To sing a sweet song in the winter's night

A mole wished for a wife
To be the sun beneath the earth

And as all those wishes pressed down on Tiny
Where she sheltered alone beneath the snow
Shivering and starving
One flake enough to smother her

As she contemplated a life
Spent underground
Amongst those who could not see
The light

Her heart shrank and hardened
Into a walnut shell
And she cursed the selfish wish
That had birthed her into life

66

But when she saw the swallow
Lying lifeless
Its song silenced
Its feathers torn
The walnut shell cracked open
Love she did not believe she possessed
Poured out
Wings resurrected
And far away, a tiny prince
In a tiny blossom
Emerged into
The first spring's
Light

Dream Garden
Jorinda and Joringel, Part Five

The witch has gathered girl-birds so long
She does not remember
If she was once a girl herself
Who gathered flowers
Plucked petals like feathers
Made wishes, dreamed of flight

Sometimes, the spell-caster tells herself a story
That might once have been truth:

A girl picked the loveliest flowers
From an enchanted garden
Petals the exact shade
Of the ocean beneath a full moon
A distant desert's red sands
The plumage of a tropical bird

The girl had never seen such sights
Never left her tiny village
Yet she recognized the colors
Vowed one day to search the world
And find them all—

But she had stolen blossoms
From the wrong garden
Dared to dream outside
The gates

The girl was cursed
By magic or
Bitter disappointment
By chance or fate

Now, the girl, grown
Old, cloaks herself in
Trees and shadows

She makes birds
That will never fly

Locks her mind tight like
A cage

Only in midnight dreams do the
Old yearnings re-awaken
The color of the ocean
The sand, the gardens
The sunlit
Sky

Thorns and Wings
The Six Swans/The Wild Swans

The girl wished she could be water
Soft, but strong
Enough to shape a stone
And feel no pain
And have no soul

She wished she could be a swan
Soaring on white wings
Trailing feathers like wishes
She'd look down, from such heights
On earthly desires like children's toys
Miles below

The girl gathered nettles from graveyards
Watched ghouls devour hearts
Her own heart stuck in her throat
So she couldn't speak
While blisters burned her fingers
Making monstrous things

Of her flesh and of the six shirts
She sewed

For six long years

As her brothers flew above her
She wove fabric of stinging nettles
And wondered:

Was she truly saving her brothers
By sacrificing herself?

Or was she digging them all a deeper trap

A grave, for why would anyone with wings
Choose to give them up? And wouldn't they
Having once known flight, feel the loss
Like day turned night?

She couldn't stop ruminating, running
Her hands over poison barbs, asking—
Was this right?

The years passed
The blisters on her hands
Branded into scars
And she forgot what it was like
To speak

All those thoughts slowed her down
So when the day came
To rest the shirts like spiked blankets on her
Brothers' backs
She wasn't done

The youngest had only half a shirt
His transformation incomplete
One swan wing remained, a question mark
Asking what it is to be human—

A gift worth suffering for, or

The curse of a clipped wing?

Part Four: Enchanted Castles

Hidden deep within the forest
Beyond the gated gardens
The stones spiked with thorns
Pinpricks of warning, of challenge and
Promise
Spires and towers
Reaching above the highest treetops
Calling to them all—

Calling the maidens in bare feet and
Tattered cloaks, fleeing
Memories they'll never
Speak, seeking to
Transform

Calling the suitors on horseback, with
Their dull swords and worn shields
Driving their weary mounts forward
Hoping resurrection
Comes

Calling the sorceresses who hide
Behind wrinkled flesh and
Withered limbs, waiting
For the right moment to
Cast their disguises
Off

Calling all who yearn to
Escape and to arrive, to
Possess and be possessed, to
Conquer and to burrow
To find home in a
Strange, dark

Place

Calling all those who gaze into the
Shadows between the branches
And see a path to traverse, a journey
Toward the castle

All those who search for something
They lost so long ago, they've forgotten
The substance beyond the ache

They know answers lie
Beyond the thorns
Beyond the stone

Deep within the castle, a hearth fire
Burns, an ensorcelled blossom, a
Throbbing red heart

A destiny for
Dreamers and desperate
Believers who, despite the
Brambles, still reach and
Reach with their
Bare arms, their
Soft, defenseless
Palms

Curse of the Firstborn
Sleeping Beauty

You were always reading stories
Of girls who did what you could not

The ones who searched for spindles, dug their
Flesh in and pierced their thumbs, emerged stronger
And bloodier and more beautiful and danced off to
New adventures, new desires while you

Lay on your childhood bed, half-asleep
Tired from homework and diets and
Exercise routines, flipping the pages of
A Frederick's of Hollywood catalog

Knowing your parents were downstairs
In separate rooms, watching separate TVs
Guarding the home, guarding your dreams
So that your mind could not dare to clothe you

In the lacy lingerie; your thoughts couldn't craft
You into something worthy of a different kind of
Attention, something more than grades and
Graduate schools, something you so desperately

Wanted to become, even if it meant possession
Even if it meant being awakened by a stranger's
Touch, his tongue, but you would have had to take the
Step, had to touch the spindle and you were a

Firstborn, coddled and protected and
Imprisoned in a world of shouldn'ts and
Couldn'ts, so you shrank and slept and
Wandered enchanted castles in

Reveries: dungeons and towers
Beasts and princes, walls weeping moisture
On stone and balustrades blooming moon
Flowers; you, cursed to make beauty with

Your words when you wanted so much to
Be beautiful in your body, wanted so much
To be a youngest daughter fleeing through
The forest, lovely in her loose-limbed

Abandon, to be the creature each demon and
Every savior yearned to consume; but no
Adventurer came to the house your parents
Guarded, no one arrived to rescue or ravish you

So you slept, and by the time you realized you could
Only wake yourself, the sickle moon had faded

The sun was dull as an old spindle

Struggling to pierce through the clouds

Skin and Salt
Donkeyskin/Cap o' Rushes/Thousandfurs

Love can be a horror
Rank as the scent of animal skin
The slip-scratch of raw leather against
Tender flesh

The hood hiding your golden hair
Your blue eyes
You breathe in a creature that
Died—

For you

An animal gave its life
To keep you concealed
Invisible
Safe
From starving eyes

Sacrifice is love
Cloaked, in a different
Guise

You must eat the meat
Even without salt, my
Dear

Dear deer

Bitter love
Invading your veins
Like the minerals from that meat
The iron makes you slow and heavy
With the weight

Of grief
But strong enough, too
To run

From one castle to another, to a land of
Gold-green fields and serene blue streams
A land where the sun shines too bright
To wear your cloak of skin
Your coat of a thousand
Creatures' fur

All the people here, in this castle where you work
In the kitchens, in the cellars—they eye you with
Suspicion

They know only a benevolent ruler, only the soft
Sun's love, caressing their bare flesh

They know only the taste of
Sweet, salted meat

They don't know the love that
Freezes and
Burns

The love you choke down your
Gagging throat

Your curse is a gift. Unlike those sun-soaked
Folk, you recognize the treasure hidden in a
Walnut shell, the ring concealed in a cake
Or soup

You know better than to trust, to swallow it
Whole. But even the wrong sort of love

Has its lessons, its
Rewards—

A ring can be hollow and
Unbroken, empty and
Entire

Like a soup without
Seasoning
A cake without
Sugar
Meat without
Salt—

Like an old cloak hung to wait
On a hook
Till the moment you must slip
Its skin back
Over yours

Eternity
The Snow Queen

I didn't really want to trek all the way to that castle made of ice
In bare feet, with no coat or hat or mittens
Just to save that stupid boy who was always so mean to me
After that mirror shard landed in his eye but even sometimes
Truth be told
Before, when we were
Innocent but not
Sweet

I didn't really want to travel so far—
There were so many places I could have stopped
Along the way
And had a perfectly nice life, or at least
A few good years

There was that cottage with the kind, old woman
Who reminded me of Kay's grandma
(Who I always wished, secretly, was my grandma)
The woman who grew flowers that told stories
And cherries so sweet they soothed all pain

If only the red-painted rose on her hat had not made me
Remember thorns
I might have stayed forever—

Then came that castle, lined with silk the color of
Thornless roses, roses so different from the old
Woman's, soft pink blossoms that would never
Fade. Soporific castle, where the princess invited
Me to sleep a sleep so long
I might never have awakened—

If she had not given me the choice, the gold

Carriage and passage to the north, I would have
Stayed. But that gold brought bright eyes my way:
A robber girl peering shrewd from the forest
Her gaze penetrating the frosted window of the carriage
Invading my insides, burrowing in my warmth

She saw the side of me that needed no
Fur coat or muff, no comb through my tangled
Locks, no boy I sought to rescue despite
His cruel words and eyes and heart

The side of me that needed only bare feet
On earth, the sounds of rustling leaves and
Burbling streams, the thrill of the hunt
Taste of stolen metal and meat, my
Robber girl beside me—

I could have stayed. I would have stayed, if it
Wasn't for the way my lover, my thief always slept
With her long, sharp knife. I knew she would never
Loosen her fist from around that wooden hilt
So I chose the snow beneath my bare feet, the
Frost cocooning my hands, while my robber
Girl dozed with her knife inside my fur muff

As I walked, I wondered: Would my cruel boy, Kay,
Always hold that glass shard in his heart, clutch it
Tight like a fist around the handle of a knife? Was I
Foolish to have left what I had left
Behind?

And when I made it past the snowflake guards, to the
Great ice palace with its piercing spires, with my numb
Hands and feet and heart, I realized just how foolish I
Had been

And when I saw the queen on her throne of ice, her beauty
Frozen and fadeless, I understood how very worthless my
Efforts were

And when I saw that stupid, mean boy, older and leaner
Now, sitting on the floor with his puzzle, trying to arrange
The pieces into a word that did not exist, I believed
We were two halves of the same whole—

Both of us reaching for what should not be reached for
Seeing what should not be seen. We might never truly
See each other, never grasp what we yearned for

The very thought of it made me weep—

Warm, salty tears that swept the glass in my Kay's
Eyes and heart away

He looked at me, his blue eyes clear and kind and cruel
And I thought:

Perhaps our puzzle pieces will never notch. Perhaps
There is no eternity, no beauty without a freeze; but
We could still walk beside each other, jagged edges
Searching for the way home

We left the frozen fortress, and the ice
Melted from our hearts, from our
Memories, as if it were
Nothing more than
A painful
Dream

Blessed Curse
The Seven Ravens

Dear, you were blessed:
The beloved daughter your parents wished for
For so long

Dear, you were cursed:
With your birth, your seven brothers
Lost their human forms

(your fault, your fault, your fault)

Dear, you were blessed:
The good stars gave you a gift
To unlock castle doors

Dear, you were cursed:
You lost the good stars' gift
And surrendered your own finger bone

(your pain, your pain, your pain)

Dear, you were blessed:
The glass castle shattered
A frosted illusion, brought down by
Your sacrifice, your blood

Dear, you were cursed:
Your brothers were restored
But you remained the girl whose life
Had never been her own

(your love, your love, your love)

Dear, you were cursed:
No prince waited, tall and strong among the glass shards
To mourn over your missing finger, order a replacement
Made of precious metal, weld you whole

Dear, you were blessed:
You gazed at the stump on your left
Hand, a hole gutted from your
Heart, made visible to all

You said

(I'm whole, I'm whole, I'm whole)

Too Late or Never
East of the Sun, West of the Moon

When you're traveling east of the sun
And west of the moon
You're always late
Racing against time
The elements and
Fate

There is no map but your body
And the marks upon it:

The raw red stripe across your wrist
Where the tallow seared you
Along with the lover you
Lost

The knots in your hair
Where the east and west and south
Winds whipped it round your face
Plastered it over your eyes
Till you were blind to all but
The storm whirring, stirring your
Insides

The blue burns where the north wind nearly
Dropped you in the cold, roiling ocean
And the water froze the tips of your
Toes

And still you clung to the back of the
Wind; you flew beyond the borders of the
World, guided only by the compass of your
Heart

Till you landed at the castle where your
Selfless love, your selfish wishes, your
Foolish errors all slept, together, waiting
For you to free them

Free him—your bear prince, brutal
Animal and gentle lover, the one you
Desired and the mirror image of
Yourself

You had slept with this tender monster
Of your heart for so long
Believing yourself blind in
Darkness, not understanding
You needed no candlelight to see

You did not learn the truth
Till you had journeyed east of the sun
And west of the moon
To the castle at the end of the world

The truth—

Only you possess the power
To rescue him, to rescue you

To wash clean the old stains, mistakes, selfish
Foolish things you had to do, the trip
You had to take—

Only you

And so you should never have worried. No
Matter how long the journey, you
Would never be too
Late

Invisible Bars
Jorinda and Joringel, Part Six

The cast of characters:

      Petrified boy
      Vengeful witch
      Feathered girl

The setting:

      Bucolic village
      Shadowed forest
      Cold castle made of stone—

      All cages
      Of a sort

Bars surrounding the players
Straitjackets defining
Their predestined paths
Their rigid roles
Leading, at last
To the denouement:

A dream of disenchantment. A stone boy's search
For a different stone, for a dew-drop pearl to undo
Wishes and curses alike

He conceals his stone within a flower, hard
Kernel within soft petals, toughened heart
Beating beneath defenseless flesh

Everything he touches

Transforms:

The witch loses her power

The birdcages' bars dissolve

The songbirds shed flawless
Feathers and become girls with
Scarred skin and voices that
Waver and croak

Jorinda stands before Joringel again, at last, after
So many years. Her auburn hair like a flame
In the sun beaming through the cracked
Castle wall. Her blue eyes brimming over
Spilling out relief. She clutches a feather
In each hand—one red, one blue. She
Holds them so tight Joringel fears she
Will never let go, just as he fears
That kernel of stone in his heart
Will never
Dissolve

(Stone fetters
Flight, after
All)

Joringel reaches for Jorinda, his legs too heavy,
two boulders, to take that final step. Jorinda's arms
Extend only so far. Her feathered hands
Soar toward the bars of a cage she
Still sees

Joringel's stone heart cracks—

An ending, a breaking

                    An opening, a beginning

Tender

            Jagged

No sorcery left to glamour

The raw edges

            Smooth

Epilogue: Disenchanted

Re-Story
Jorinda and Joringel, Part Seven

Seven pages preserved from a
Storybook, the rest long
Lost

A young girl folds each paper sheet
Into the shape of a bird
Dangles them from strings above her bed
Arranging wings in false flight

The same girl, older now
Refuses to let reminders of
Past dreams hang over her each
Night. She gives the birds true
Flight:

One she places in a rosebush, one a
Birch tree, one a river she hopes will
Carry it all the way to the salty sea

Soon all seven have flown

The girl grows older still, tries to forget
The words of that story, just as the print on the
Paper-birds has surely dissolved—

Dissolved, but only to return through
The currents of wind and time

Invisible wings flying back to the girl
Entering through her open lips
Dancing around her ribcage

Slipping inside her bloodstream

Restored to the living vessel
That has been theirs
All along

Uncaged

I spent my childhood bent over books
Tracing the words with my eyes, my hands and
Heart, till those words leapt off the page
Transplanted themselves beneath
My skin, a secret tattoo

I grew older, and those words stiffened
To stone, enchanted as if by some witch
They hardened and hemmed me in

My heart, protected behind stories of
Perfect princesses and noble princes
Sacrifice and suffering always rewarded
With true, unsullied love

Why bother with real life
When it could never, ever
Live up?

My heart, behind those bars
Sprouted feathers that grew into wings
A songbird that beat itself against the bones
Of my ribcage, desperate, so desperate
For someone to witness its
Pain

Like a nightingale in a castle
No human inhabited
Singing its voice raw
Notes echoing off stone walls
Swallowed into the endless
Dark

Eventually, inevitably

That songbird heart transformed
Chiseled with desire
Carved into a key that
Turned a lock—

And cracked my cage. Another
Spell set into motion, wished for and
Feared at once. A bird born in
Darkness, too suddenly
Thrust into light

My bird-heart danced with the frenzy of a moth
Drawn closer, closer, closer to a
Flame bright enough to
Burn its feathers
Off—

And without those feathers, there
Was no lovely enchanted
Songbird, no pure
Princess, just me:

An ordinary girl
With a sore heart
And a map of words
Beneath my skin

Words that had been
Cage, burden, reckless
Hope

Now became the only
Map that could guide me

Away from
                    The witches' castles

                    The illusionists' gardens
                    The strange creatures' forests
And back home—

Home
To the only sorcery
I needed:

The wings/
          words/
                power/
                      love
Blooming from
My tender, fertile
Broken
        but
Mended

Heart.

The Question

Once upon a time
There was a girl who wanted so badly to be loved
She made every mistake it was possible to make

She traveled into dark and dangerous places—

                —fairy-tale forests, claustrophobic
                nightclubs, Craigslist personal ads—

She offered herself to any clutching hands—

                —the calloused grip of a blacksmith,
                the manicured fingers of a businessman,
                a witch's bony claws—

And if she came across a boy kind enough
To wait, to withhold his embrace till she reached out first—

She ran

The girl made a fool of herself. She begged
For attention. She expected too much
And too little
At once

For a while, she thought she'd received
What she desired
Attracted men who admired
Her body

So she looked for the imperfections
On her own flesh
The reasons she didn't deserve this

And she always found them

So the girl retreated
To the blank page
Where she could list her flaws
And her foolish transgressions
And relive them a million times

Still, it wasn't punishment enough

She had to keep writing
Rewriting
Remembering
The tales she had read once
About fantasy and desire
She had to ask herself the question
She had avoided for so long:

Can I love those stories, live those stories
In a world without fairies and witches
Spells and enchantments
A world where happily-ever-after
Isn't what you thought?

Can I still be a heroine
When I've been stupid and selfish
Ugly and foolish
The witch and the princess
The light and the dark?

The Answer

She could.

Because she had to.

Because this world
Is the only one we've got.

Because magic
Has many definitions

And fantasy
Is its own kind of truth.

Because, by reading and retelling
And reliving
The stories of so many heroines—

Women who had been brave and foolish
Kind and selfish
Patient and impetuous
Living love and loss—

Through these stories
She lives to tell how
She found
The heroine within
Herself.

Notes on Previous Publications

Several of these poems have previously appeared online, including:

"When Everything Else Was Gone" and "Strange Creatures" in *The Silent World in Her Vase*,
"Red Hood in the Wood" in *Sledgehammer Lit*,
"Clawed Creatures" in *From the Farther Trees*,
"Poissonnier" in *Gastropoda*,
"Little Houses" in *Nymph*,
"Little Bones" in *The Raven Review*,
"Marlene" and "Skin and Salt" in *Punk Noir*,
"Gretel" in *Tangled Locks Journal*,
"No Dumb Bunny" (as "Sanctuary") in *The Elpis Pages*,
"The House on Chicken Legs" in *Janus Literary*,
"Snegurochka" and "Rampion" in *Crow & Cross Keys*,
"Amphibious Love" in *Second Chance Lit*,
"Thorns and Wings" (as "The Wild Swans") in *Carmina Magazine*,
"Salt and Stone" (as "The Maiden Without Hands") in *Lunette Review*,
"Curse of the Firstborn" in *Roi Faineant Press*,
"Eternity" in *Lover's Eye Press*,
"Uncaged" in *The Amphibian*,
"The Question" and "The Answer" in *Indian Feminist Review*.